WHAT PEOPLE ARE SAYING /

DANCING WITH NEM

"For those of us upon the Druid path, Nemetona is an intriguing goddess. Joanna's book welcomes us into Nemetona's sanctuary that we might know her more intimately. With a combination of helpful exercises and the gentle but compelling wisdom born of Joanna's relationship with this goddess, we discover that the concept of the Grove and the experience of Sacred is more rich and complex than we imagined."
Philip Carr-Gomm, author of *The Druid Way* and *Druid Mysteries: Ancient Wisdom for the 21st Century.*

"This lovely volume teaches us how to re-sacralise our life. In a sad and violent world we need to remember to find the sacred within all things; our room, our hearth, our home, our altar, our garden, and our sacred Grove. By doing this, ultimately we will find the sacred within all creatures; animal, mineral, plant and human. This is the lesson of Nemetona, divine protectress of the sacred enclosure, so wonderfully expressed within this book."
Ellen Evert Hopman, author of *Priestess of the Forest – A Druid Journey, The Druid Isle, Priestess of the Fire Temple – A Druid's Tale* and other volumes. www.elleneverthopman.com

"An incisive and insightful treatise on the subject of sacred space; and one that explores the often overlooked dance of ever-changing boundaries between the self and the not-self. A worthy addition to anyone's library."
Graeme K Talboys, author of the *Druid Way Made Easy*, and *The Path Through the Forest: A Druid Guidebook.*

"How we handle sacred space may feel like one of those abstract, spiritual matters only the most dedicated Pagan needs to get into. Joanna van der Hoeven explores the real life, real world importance of knowing where your edges are and understanding how that impacts on your relationships. This is a book that demonstrates the pragmatic importance of being spiritually awake. Innovative, gently challenging and full of ideas for things you can do, this is an excellent book for anyone who wishes to deepen their spiritual practice. The ideas here would work perfectly well for any Pagan, and are especially relevant to Druids. A helpful, thoughtful book, I hope this represents the future of Druid writing as we shift away from broad brush introductions to look deeply at facets of practice and thinking. Highly recommended."

Nimue Brown, author of *Druidry and Meditation, Druidry and the Ancestors,* and other volumes. www.druidlife.wordpress.com

"Dancing with Nemetona is engrossing in its simplicity, leading the reader easily down paths that seem welcoming and familiar... until you realise that the hidden complexities mask the Lady Herself, who has been with you all along.

"Joanna's voice carries the impact and knowledge of the ancestors, combined with the wisdom of contemporary understanding. The beauty of her words merges spiritual feeling and practical activity, drawing the reader into greater understanding of both the Goddess and themselves, no matter what path they may choose to walk. A true gem, which I shall be glad to return to again and again."

Cat Treadwell, Druid Priest and author of *A Druid's Tale* and *Facing the Darkness.*

"A rare treat! As always with the workings of the Lady I fell into conversation with Joanna van der Hoeven by "accident" ... of course, there's no such a thing when we touch threads with others on the path. This book speaks to my heart; it gives an excellent way of finding and following one's path. Although

Joanna walks the way of Druidry this book is not exclusive, you do not have to be a Druid to dance with Nemetona; indeed the book is deeply inclusive and allowing. The exercises and insights she offers call one's spirit to the surface and engender a deeper knowing of oneself.

"Joanna's language is delightful, it lights up the heart with joy, enchanting you to dance with the goddess. She is an enchantress, a sacred singer.

"*Dancing with Nemetona* will go onto the bookshelf by my bed and likely become dog-eared as I'll be dipping into it often to be refreshed and enchanted. It will go on my Kindle so that when I'm out camping in the woods I can lie in my hammock of an evening and read while the owls sing in the trees around me."
Elen Sentier, author of *Celtic Chakras* and *Elen of the Ways: British Shamanism – Following the Deer Trods*.

"Nemetona has been, until recently, a goddess obscured by the passing of time. Joanna's lovely book gives the reader an entry point into the sacred space that Nemetona embodies, enabling us to touch upon her deeper aspects. With each chapter, Joanna fleshes out the bones of this historically elusive goddess, allowing her to grow before our eyes into an accessible and approachable presence, as close and familiar to us as the homes we dwell in and the bodies we inhabit."
Maria Ede-Weaving, *A Druid Thurible Blog*.

Pagan Portals

Dancing with Nemetona

A Druid's Exploration of Sanctuary and Sacred Space

Pagan Portals

Dancing with Nemetona

A Druid's Exploration of
Sanctuary and Sacred Space

Joanna van der Hoeven

MOON
BOOKS

Winchester, UK
Washington, USA

First published by Moon Books, 2014
Moon Books is an imprint of John Hunt Publishing Ltd., Laurel House, Station Approach,
Alresford, Hants, SO24 9JH, UK
office1@jhpbooks.net
www.johnhuntpublishing.com
www.moon-books.net

For distributor details and how to order please visit the 'Ordering' section on our website.

Text copyright: Joanna van der Hoeven 2013

ISBN: 978 1 78279 327 4

A CIP catalogue record for this book is available from the British Library.

Design: Stuart Davies
www.stuartdaviesart.com

Printed and bound by CPI Group (UK) Ltd, Croydon, CR0 4YY

We operate a distinctive and ethical publishing philosophy in all
areas of our business, from our global network of authors to
production and worldwide distribution.

CONTENTS

Acknowledgements

This book is dedicated to Nemetona, my patron goddess who I have come to know and love over the years. Held within her embrace, transformed by her teachings, I am ever thankful. Long may we dance together, my Lady of the Sacred Grove!

Introduction

Nemetona; Goddess of the Sacred Grove. It conjures up an image of a great, sacred space within a mythic wood, surrounded by nature and sanctified by it. Hers is a name that has survived throughout the ages with mystery.

Very little is known about the goddess Nemetona. We have a few inscriptions found at sacred spots, such as at Altripp, Trier, and Eisenberg in Germany. There is also an inscription to her at Bath, Somerset, in the United Kingdom – indeed, there are several inscriptions to various gods at Bath, as well as to the Roman legion and the nature or deva spirits of place. She was also known in Gaul, where the Treveri tribe originated, as we can tell from her inscription at Bath. There was also a tribe called the Nemetes (People of the Sacred Grove). It's not known whether Nemetona was their tutelary goddess or not, but it is not beyond the realm of possibility. In Spain we find the Nemetatae, a tribe mentioned by Ptolemy.

So, though we have little in the way of knowing the goddess Nemetona apart from seeing her name in inscriptions, Nemetons (sacred groves, sacred spaces) can be found throughout the Celtic world by the name. In the Greek colony of Massilia, now Marseilles, there is a reference to Nemeton. In Gaul, we have Augustonemeton, Nemetacum or Nemetocerna Atrebatum, Nemetobriga, Nemetatarum, Nemetodurum and Nemossus.

Britain also hosts a number of sites that contain the word nemeton: Nemetostatio in North Tawton, Vernemetum in Willoughby, and Medionemeton.

Nemetona has been paired up with several gods on different inscriptions, though whether this is referring to them as a "couple" or not is not known. She has been linked to Mars, Mercury and Loucetious in various places.

The root of the name Nemetona is from the Celtic *Nemeto* –

sacred place or sanctuary, as can been seen in the Old Irish Nemed. The Nemedians were also the third mythic invaders of early Ireland and settled in Northern Ireland. In Wales, the equivalent is Nyfed (sacred grove) but is no longer used, having been replaced by Llan, meaning "wooded enclosure". You will find many place names beginning with Llan in Wales.

This is pretty much all that we have to go on when it comes to this elusive goddess. Her attributes were not written down anywhere, her rites or rituals never recorded. And yet She seems to have been quite popular. We can only imagine why this is so – perhaps at one point She was so popular that it just wasn't required, as She existed in the hearts and minds of people in everyday life. Or perhaps She was always an elusive goddess; we will never know.

This book is a personal exploration of the goddess Nemetona. With what little history we have, it is up to us to seek Her out and find Her again, making our own connections. Within these pages are ways in which I have come to know Her, and in which you may as well, if you have not already met with Her. What is found in these pages is not long-standing tradition, but my own journeys of discovery with this goddess that I wish to share with you.

May you be inspired, and may you find peace within the sacred grove.

Chapter One

Lady of Boundaries and Edges

"Know thyself", the ancient Oracle of Delphi said. Through investigating and searching our edges and boundaries, we come to know both ourselves and Nemetona. In defining our edges, we know where we can expand and contract, and where we can let go completely into her embrace.

"The Edge... there is no honest way to explain it because the only people who really know where it is, are the ones who have gone over." – Hunter S Thompson.

Nemetona is the Goddess of Edges, teaching us where our edges meet and connect with others. Through her we learn how to interact with honour in the world, and how to engage with every other living thing in respect and dignity.

When I first began delving into Druidry, I was taught how to find where my edges were. Some people liken it to your aura, that space around you that still holds your energy without a physical form. In Druidry, we call this the nemeton, named after the goddess of these sacred spaces. Our nemeton is that space within which we would not allow any but those with whom we are most intimately acquainted – a lover, a child, a close friend, a cat. Each person's nemeton is different. They can be any shape or colour, and extend or contract to any size.

When we are born, we live inside our mother's nemeton, and even our father's, from the time of conception until perhaps the age of two years old. Once we have achieved this age, we begin to test our own boundaries, and those of our parents. We are able to move about with a yearning to learn new things, to experience the world and sometimes forgetting that link to our mother or father, only to turn back to a parent when we fall down, or come across something we cannot understand, or find difficult or frightening.

We continue to drift away from our parent or parents' nemeton as we grow up, and upon reaching the age of when we start primary school, another shift takes place. We spend an entire day away from our parents and learn to find new relationships with new quasi-parental figures, such as our teachers. These people we assume are supposed to nurture us and help us along our path and, if we are lucky, they do so with love, compassion and a great degree of skill without actually substituting the parents themselves. It's a daunting task, and just one of the many reasons that good teachers will stay with us for our entire lives.

Our sense of self, our nemeton, changes again in our teenage years, when we yearn for that separation, to be independent without the full knowledge of all that it entails. We push against our parents' nemetons, challenging them constantly, as we have yet to discover our own. We are in the starting stages of defining and declaring our sense of self; our nemeton is in constant change and flux as much as we are: hormonally, idealistically and mentally.

By the time we leave home, our nemetons may be firmly established, or not, depending upon the individual. We may always continue to have a link to our parents, yet that chord is gossamer thin, to allow us to be our own person – anything other than that could feel smothering, over-protective and unwelcome.

In our thirties and forties is when we feel we begin to really understand who and what we are in this life. Our nemetons now become firmly established, and unless we learn how to see and adapt to them, very bad habits can form.

Our fifties and sixties are liberating years for many, especially for women, some of whom no longer feeling so attached to that dreaded bugbear of aging. This is a similar time to that of the teenager for the nemeton – it can crack apart at this time and we can gleefully put it back together however we so desire, for we know we now have the power to do so.

I as yet have no experience of the nemeton for those aged seventy and above – but I would assume that it would be a process of fully knowing just who we are after reflecting upon the life that we have led, and either feeling joy or happiness at the person we have become, or knowing that we never had any idea in the first place! At any rate, I can be pretty certain that at any age, it is never too late to change, should you so wish…

Learning to see and feel your nemeton and those of others takes some practice, but once gained is a skill that never goes away, and which is most beneficial in creating and sustaining honourable relationships. An easy way to begin is to look at a houseplant, or a sleeping cat – something which isn't going to move around too much. Look an inch or so around the edges of the object of your meditation, and then look through that to the wall or area beyond. If you softly let go of your focus, you will start to see an outer line that shimmers around the actual object. You can then take this to other objects, and other people. This space between the edge of that line and the object of your choice may have a certain colour, vibration, or even sound. It may be any shape or any size. It may have large holes in it, be opaque or totally transparent. It may be tinged with crackling energy or cooling like a mountain stream.

Look down at your hands and see your own nemeton. Or, stand in front of a mirror and perform the same exercise as you would with any other object. Notice the shape, size, colour, even scent of your own nemeton.

Our personal nemetons will change their appearance according to our current lives and how good we become at using them intentionally. If we are unaware of our nemeton, then we often find we clash with other people, or have a hard time connecting with others, or withdraw into ourselves so much that others may pass us by when we would like them to acknowledge us. Conscious manipulation of our nemeton can indeed change the way we feel about ourselves and how we are perceived. As with everything in Druidry, this must be done with honour and integrity.

It takes work to be aware of your nemeton, and how to change it accordingly. If, say, we are visiting someone in hospital, then we may wish to present our nemeton as one of healing. We may go up to their bed, and open our nemeton to theirs, allowing them into our space for a while, providing that sanctuary that they may need for however short a period of time. They may smile, welcome our presence, and be uplifted by our visit. This is because we have, in trust, opened ourselves to them, and allowed them to see how much we really do care about them, and how we wish them to be better, or more at ease.

When dealing with animals, it is invaluable to be aware of your own nemeton and how to adjust it, if necessary. Different animals will react in a myriad of ways to your natural nemeton. If you are a high energy person, with a high energy nemeton, then high energy dogs will run up to you from across the playing field just to be with you. If you are walking out in the forest with the same energy and come across a herd of deer, they will react in the opposite way, running away from that bright energy. Children, birds, horses and cats are very sensitive to the nemeton of any adult.

Opening our nemeton requires a level of ability and trust. We close ourselves off on so many levels each and every day simply because of the sensory overload that we are exposed to through people, media and more. We have so many demands on our life that if a stranger came up to us in need after a hectic day, we may shut ourselves off completely from them and not provide the help that they might need, however simple and genuine their request may be. Our cat may come to us for a cuddle and we don't even notice, as we are too busy distracting ourselves with television and high fat food. We switch off constantly, and we must relearn how not to do this, and instead be aware and mindful of our nemeton and how it interacts with others.

I am writing on the computer upstairs, my fingers clacking the keyboard in the late evening sunshine. I vaguely hear my husband's car as he drives up the street and into the driveway. Absorbed in my work, I don't really hear the front door opening. He shouts "Hello!" as he enters – I mumble something incoherently as I try to keep my train of thought and the words spreading out onto the white computer screen in front of me. He comes up the stairs and I don't even hear that. He enters the room, kissing my right cheek, then my left. His nemeton extends to wrap itself around me. And yet I withdraw, fully engaged in writing, my nemeton snapping shut. He kisses the right side of my neck, then the left, and I am barely able to refrain from sighing aloud in frustration as I need to finish this piece. My nemeton, unbeknownst to me now, sends sparks of shooting energy, pushing him away. He kisses me once more, I cannot even remember where now, and then goes to sit on the bed where the cat has come in to greet him. I continue typing, getting it out, needing a last little bit of concentration. I have no knowledge yet of how I have dishonoured him and myself, and even the cat.

As he sits on the bed and fusses the cat, I turn around and see his nemeton, a little wounded, withdrawn around his chest. But as he scratches the cat, and sees the bliss on her face, his soul opens to her little soul and once again his nemeton is where it should be, open and joyous in his own home. I apologise and stop typing, coming over to sit within his arms while together we stroke the cat and share in the embrace of Nemetona.

Exercise in Utilising your Nemeton

Sit or stand in a comfortable spot. You have already completed previous exercises in looking at your own nemeton and those of other objects. Become aware, if you are not already, of your own nemeton. Find out where the edges are, how soft or sharp they are, what colour your nemeton currently is.

Now take a deep breath, and upon exhaling try to expand

your nemeton a little bit. Relax, and with each exhale, spread it out a little more until you have encompassed an area you are comfortable with. Maintain this for a few more breaths and then, upon inhaling, breathe your nemeton back into yourself.

Experiment with changing the colour of your nemeton, or the coolness or warmth of it. Make it transparent or opaque. Try to fill in any holes if you find any.

Our own personal nemeton is a very sacred space, a space that is honoured and this reflects the goddess Herself. She resides both within us and without, and we must always remember to live with honour and integrity for both ourselves and for Her. Utilising your nemeton for selfish gain, for power-tripping or other negative uses is simply bad form – our behaviour reflects our souls. While we cannot control the behaviour of others, our own must shine with integrity as much as we can. We all are simply doing the best we can at every given moment.

Honour and Awareness of the Nemeton

As stated above, the nemeton is a sacred and holy space. When we interact with others, we must always bear this in mind. Using our nemeton to gain attention needlessly or simply to get what we want is dishonouring ourselves, others and the goddess.

We must honour the nemeton of others as much as we honour our own. They are all sacred. By discovering where our edges lie, we can also learn to see where and how other nemetons work and, in doing so, work honourably with them.

Standing just beyond the canopy of bare branches, I call to the spirit of the ancient oak, "Spirit of Oak, Guardian Spirit of Place, I come with honour, peace and respect. May I share in your nemeton?" A soft breeze ruffles through my hair, moving the last of the dried leaves still clinging to the branches. I look to the nemeton of the oak, a soft shimmering indigo in the fading light. I feel a shift, a sense of opening and know that I am welcomed beneath its boughs. "Thank you," I whisper.

I move to sit with my back against the huge trunk, closing my eyes and listening to the sounds of blackbirds and owls in the growing dusk. I can feel my nemeton relaxing, expanding. The tree's nemeton sleepily wraps around my own, and I feel the warmth of its embrace, listening to its songs of water and sunlight, of the long winter's dreaming to come. My nemeton sings back to it, lullabies of rest and slumber, and together we simply are, in the falling dark.

It is easy for forget that everything has its own nemeton – not simply other humans. Too often we can slip into another's nemeton and not be aware of it. We may have some sense of foreboding, a deep unease in certain areas. If we search for the source, we may come to understand it and better adjust our own nemeton in response.

This ancient oak woodland has called to me for years. I know that I am now trespassing, the current landowners suddenly deciding to cut off all access, even though very few people came here anyway. I grumbled at their decision, and queried their intention. I was going to go no matter what.

When I came upon the vast oaks, I asked permission to enter. I neither heard nor felt a response. Unsure, I called again, and again I received no answer. I went in anyway.

Walking up to an ancient oak, split open many years ago by lightning but still alive, I called to it. Again there was no response. I laid my hand upon the bark, and suddenly in my mind a loud "GO AWAY!" resounded. I stepped back, bewildered, and tried again. This time the tree's energy retreated so fully into itself as to be imperceptible, and also calling to the other trees to do the same. They all withdrew, and I stood there, unsure as to what to do.

They clearly did not want me there, for whatever reason. I bowed my head and apologised for intruding, and quickly left.

Some beings may not want to interact with us. Cats will certainly let us know when they've had enough and when they want to be left alone. Can you imagine how hard it is for a stationary being, such as a tree or a rock, a mountain or a forest, to convey that message to those who won't listen? We must always be aware of both our own nemeton and that of others.

I had said something that she didn't agree with. Her nemeton instantly shifted, and old hurts and pain came forth, blazing her edges with red spiky energy. I felt my own nemeton instantly shift in response, becoming a dark opaque colour, not allowing any of her energy in. Taking a deep breath, knowing that if I remained closed off, we wouldn't get anywhere, I consciously lightened my nemeton, turning it a pale blue, and softened the edges, feeling where they touched hers so close to mine. I smiled.

"I think we have misunderstood each other," I said, relaxing my edges even more.

Her nemeton faded to a soft pink, the spikes receding. She exhaled, and smiled in return. "Let's talk about it."

Whilst we can shift and change our own nemeton, to attempt to do so with that of another is dishonourable to say the least. All we can do is to be aware of our own edges, and hopefully others will respond with the same respect that we give them. If not, then it is up to us to respectfully withdraw.

It is also important to have these carefully delineated boundaries if we are to work with others in any way. By not being aware of your own boundaries, people can knowingly or unknowingly take advantage of you and of your openness. If we open ourselves without boundaries, we also open ourselves to the possibility of abuse, whether it is mental, physical or sexual. We must become fully aware of ourselves again in order to act accordingly with others, in full awareness and with respect.

Becoming aware of your edges is only the beginning to coming to an understanding of this sacred goddess. Once we know where our edges are, we can also be freed of them in the right environment – however, that is discussion for another chapter.

Chapter Two

Lady of Hearth and Home

It has been a long and challenging day at work. I drive home, the windows open and the radio off, fully immersing myself in the act of driving, leaving behind what happened at work and becoming entirely aware of the present moment. I feel the sandy roads beneath the wheels, the smell of the newly ploughed fields lifting my heart and filling my nostrils with that sweet, earthy scent. The village finally comes into view, the thirty mile an hour speed restriction delineating the edges of this space that I call home, and I slow down, driving under the speed limit through the little street past the village shop and post office, turning into my road.

The tyres crunch the rocks in my driveway, and I park the car, switching off the engine. I take a deep breath and look at my home, smiling. Mindfully, I open the car door and grab my handbag, closing the door shut behind me and walking towards the front door of my home, focusing on each and every step that brings me closer to Her. I take my keys out and with intent, turn the key in the lock and enter the porch, softly closing the door behind me. I take off my shoes and hang up my coat and then open the main door to the house.

My soul opens of its own accord, my own nemeton relaxing and expanding so that it merges with the physical space of the house itself, with Her. I place my hand on the door lintel and whisper a prayer, "Thank you My Lady for this sacred place, this haven of four walls and for providing me with a home. I am truly honoured." I feel the acceptance and smile, entering the home fully, saying hello to the cats and dropping my keys in the bowl.

Our homes are often places of comfort and rest, if we feel inspired by Her to make them so and if we are attuned with Her energy. We must first have some sort of idea of who we are, in order to express both ourselves and Her in our homes, creating a sense of calm, well-being and a nurturing environment. We cannot simply emulate what we think looks nice in a book or a magazine; we must feel in our body, in our blood and in our mind that this is a reflection of what our vision of hearth and home is for us.

It will be different for each person. Everyone has different views on aesthetics, décor, and arrangement. Everyone has different budgets and limitations. Everyone has different energies and inspirations and abilities to make these things manifest. What we must try to do is to create that sense of welcoming when we walk in the door, to connect with Nemetona in our homes and to honour Her for all that She provides.

Too often we can take our homes for granted. Whether it is a little apartment on the wrong side of the tracks, or a narrowboat on a canal, a country cottage near the sea or a Victorian terraced two-up, two-down construction, we must always remember that these are providing us with a space where we can relax and feel safe; it is a place that provides us shelter. Without our homes we would be exposed to the elements, and much more. We should be thankful each and every night that we have a roof over our heads – this is easily remembered when you hear the winter wind howling outside and rattling the windows, but should equally be remembered on long and lazy summer nights. It is cultivating an awareness, of being mindful of your home when you are in it and when you are not, that is key.

For some, their ideas of home may not have been places of rest, of healing and of sanctuary – they may not have been safe places. Broken homes and families may lie in their past, though they may still be filled with a longing for the safety of home. Whatever our past has brought to our present, we can still create our homes in honour of Nemetona if we only open ourselves to Her and are willing to listen.

If you are in a home that is unsafe, or any situation that is unsafe, then please do seek the appropriate help immediately.

Sitting on my meditation cushion, I hear the wind whistling past the window, the sleet slashing across the glass. The candle on my altar flickers, the incense sending out tendrils of fluid smoke around photos, fetishes and other things dear to my heart that rest upon my altar at that moment. I see one of my cats padding in, and hear the central heating turning itself on. I take a deep breath and sink further into the bones of this house, my very being seeping into every wall, every empty space, furniture and possessions. My cat climbs into my lap, and I breathe, paying attention to the stillness and the activity of the house around me, awake and aware to all that She is.

A house is not a home until you can feel Her energy within it, until you acknowledge the energies that you and others have created within those four walls that are steeped with them. It is not in the decoration of the house that makes it a home, but the feel, the energy that lies within and what you do with it that matters most.

I grew up in a small bungalow on the edge of a village in Quebec, Canada. The land was bought by my parents and the house built – there were a few houses on the street, but not all the plots had sold. Slowly they were all built upon, and we had neat little rows of houses on our cul de sac, a friendly neighbourhood with lots of children.

That little bungalow is so very dear to my heart. I grew up there, and learned many life lessons in that house and the surrounding area. My laughter is in those walls, as are my tears. The energy of my entire family fills that space with love and nurturing energy. We fought and argued in that little space, but we always knew that we were safe within it. We hugged and we ate our meals in that kitchen for twenty years or more, and still do to this day when we are all gathered together, forty years on.

I have a very strong attachment to that house. As a child, it was a safe place. We never locked our doors when we were home, and it was safe to play outside around the house, in the neighbours' yards and down the street at the playground without parental supervision. We knew the rules regarding strangers but had very little, if any, opportunity to use that knowledge, for we were very lucky growing up where we did.

I explored every nook and cranny of that house, and knew it like the back of my hand. The same applied to the garden, and even the street – I can remember to this day every crack in the asphalt of the road where we cycled up and down, where the puddles always formed and where the ants nested in the sandy verges. I can still smell the dankness of the basement, with its cool and sometimes moist walls deep within the ground. I can smell the kitchen, in fact the whole smell of the house as you walked in the door; it was not a particular scent, like sandalwood or cookies – it was the scent of home.

When my sister finally moved out of our shared bedroom and into a room downstairs I was elated – I had a room all to myself. I made this MY room – within it I could let my soul expand. I could listen to the music that I wanted to, play with the toys I wanted to play with, have some quiet time to read when I wanted to and to look out of the window and talk to the birch tree while the sun set over the hills beyond. I could be me, there in that room.

Often as we grow up our bedrooms are uniquely protected and loved as our own spaces, something that we will defend with Keep Out signs or paint our favourite colour, no matter how much our parents don't like it. It is often our first expressions of our selves, as we journey to find our selves. Posters of rock stars plastered all over the walls, or every available surface littered with unicorns – our room was a tangible expression of our very being, in the process of being and in the process of becoming. In that space, we were allowed to simply be.

If we are blessed with parents who are able to take care of us in a loving and nurturing environment, then it is they who first provide us with this physical place that we call home. It is an area where we feel safe, where we can explore with assurance that we will not venture too far from the protective circle of our parents' embrace.

We begin to explore the home as we begin to crawl, and later walk; our parents providing a safe place where we can begin to develop our senses of taste, touch, smell and sight. We learn where we are allowed to go and where we are not – where the dangerous places are, such as the stairs and the fireplace.

When we are old enough, slowly our parents remove the restrictions as to where we are able to go, allowing us the freedom to try the stairs, to go into the basement without super-vision. We get to know our home on such a personal level at that age, for we are so much closer to it, simply through our physical sensations – we touch, taste, smell, feel and truly see everything with much more focus. We lose that focus as we become older, desiring more stimulation than what we think our house can provide.

Those spaces where we can be true to ourselves, where we can find the safety and security to be ourselves, or to engage in the process of discovery of ourselves is what Nemetona provides. We create little havens in our world all the time, and with an awareness of what we are doing, we can connect more fully to this goddess.

Making a home a safe place, somewhere where we can expand our own soul song deep into the bricks and mortar of a place can be done with intention, to create a wonderful relationship to this goddess. Even if you only have a single room in the home, you can still dedicate that room to Her if you so wish, to create a space of sanctuary for yourself that you can call home.

Here are some suggestions that you can use to make your home a place dedicated to Nemetona; a place that allows you the freedom to be yourself.

- At the entrance way, perhaps on the step or on a door

frame, write or carve Her name. For a less visible option, you can write Her name in your favourite scented oil blend, which if on darkened wood or plastic should not leave a noticeable mark. Whenever you enter your home, you can touch this part of the entrance to your personal sanctuary, and say a quiet prayer that attunes you to the energy of the home and which allows your own soul to grow.

- Reconnect with your child self and explore your house fully. Get on your hands and knees and see what the living room looks like from this angle, or stand on the bed and touch the ceiling. Smell the furniture – it sounds crazy, but try it! Sit in the middle of your kitchen floor. Crawl into the attic. Touch everything. Notice how the light plays on the walls at certain points in the day, watch it move.

- Meditate in every single room – even the bathroom! Let yourself simply "be" in each and every room of your house.

- Create an altar to Nemetona in your home – find a place that you love and that you want to spend time in. This could be on the mantle of your fireplace, or a spare bedroom. Anywhere where you feel you can light a candle, maybe some incense, and allow yourself the time to expand your soul space, where you can sink into the walls and floors and feel Her energy all around you is a good space.

A Ritual House Blessing/Dedication

Clean your house from top to bottom. Really clean it – dust the blinds, mop the floors, polish the wood if necessary. Even this act can be done in the name of Nemetona, with a floor or surface cleaner made up of rosemary, water and vinegar, scented with your favourite oils – good ones that I associate with Her are patchouli, sandalwood and neroli (or a combination of all three, which is divine). After cleaning the house, take a ritual cleansing bath or purification of your choice if you so wish.

Gather together some incense or a smudge stick – sage, mugwort or rosemary are good if you prefer smudging. You can also substitute a candle in a colour of your choice if you prefer or if you are unable to work with smoke. Starting from the entrance to your home, waft the smoke or hold aloft the candle, holding in your inner vision the smoke or light sinking into every crevice of that room. Expand your own energy to blend with that of the smoke or candle's light, and recite a short prayer to Nemetona, saying these or similar words: *"Lady of hearth and home, blessed sanctuary, know that you are honoured. I dedicate/bless this space in your name, may there be peace both within and without."*

After taking the smoke or candle to each room, sit in front of your altar if you have one, or in a room where you are most comfortable. Take a moment to settle yourself, and then simply be in the moment, in your home, with the arms of the goddess all around you. Listen to the walls or floorboards creak, or the children playing outside. Feel the still air around you on your skin. Smell the scents and open your eyes to gaze around you, taking in every detail. Inhale slowly a long, deep breath, and then exhale with equal attention.

Now feel your own nemeton, that area around your personal body that you call your own, into which none but those with whom you are the most intimate are allowed in. Expand your nemeton until it fills the entire room, and then expand it further until it fills the whole house. Let it settle into the walls, melting, blending in with it. If you so desire, expand that to the area outside of your house – your gardens, the driveway, the front lawn. Stop where the borders of your land lie. Breathe in the cool, soft energy of Nemetona, then exhale into your expanded nemeton that same energy, really seeing it sink into the boundaries of your space.

Once you have delineated your area and sanctified it to your satisfaction, bow your head slightly in thanks to the goddess for her gifts.

This blessing/dedication can be done once or twice a year, to help establish the boundaries of hearth and home, and to reconnect the threads to Her if you feel that any have been dropped in the warp and weft of life.

Chants and Songs for the Lady of Hearth and Home

These chants can be performed during the dedication/blessing above, or in meditation, or even when doing the dishes! They help to reaffirm the connection between you and the home that you can feel safe in, a place where you can sleep and love, cook food and go to the loo in relative peace and security. They can be chanted or sung in thanks for all these gifts and more.

Lady of the hearth and home
In my blood and in my bones
Spirit to spirit I honour you
And in doing so honour myself too

Nemetona, Nemetona
Lady of perfect grace
Nemetona, Nemetona
Held in your embrace

Spirit of the hearth and home
You are honoured here
With gifts of love and gifts of song
With intention clear
Lady, Lady, Nemetona
Arms encircling
In my heart and in my home
May there be peace within

Sanctuary is being free
Sanctuary is being me
Sanctuary is being free
Sanctuary is being me
Gathering our energy we are
Where we're meant to be

Chapter Three

Lady of the Sacred Grove

The Celtic people, on the whole, generally did not build enclosed temples but celebrated out of doors, within the sanctity of nature. It is widely believed that the name of the goddess, Nemetona, means the Lady of the Sacred Grove. In old Irish, the word "nemed" means a sacred place, a sanctuary. The Celto-Germanic tribe, the Nemetes (People of the Sacred Grove) may have invoked her as their tutelary deity. From northern Spain, there are also the Nemetatae, a tribe from the Val de Nebro.

Thus, many people believe that the Druids, the priest caste in Celtic society, performed their rituals out of doors in sacred groves, which is where modern Druidry derives the term nemeton from for their sacred space.

Druids, and indeed many Pagans, feel very connected to nature, and very comfortable within it. Nature is perceived as sacred. As such, the whole of nature is a temple, whether it be a corner in your backyard, a part of a city park or a national forest stretching for hundreds of miles. When using the term "nature" in this chapter, I refer to that which is not of human construction. I realise that humanity is a part of nature, and cannot exist outside of it, but for the sake of ease and flow, nature will mean the natural world, the natural environment.

Though there is a lack of standing structures in which to see when and where Nemetona was worshipped, we can look to place names across Europe to see where links may still be found. In the south of France in the area of Marseilles is a reference to a nemeton where several images of the gods were supposedly placed in stone. Throughout Gaul, there are place names such as Augustonemeton in Clermont-Ferrand, in the Auvergne region of central France; Nemetocerna Atrebatum in Arras, Northern

France; in the Vallée de la Seine there is Nemetodurum, on the Plaine de la Beauce Nemossus (modern day Nemours) and Vernemetum, which is known as Vernantes on the Loire.

In Britain other place names make reference to this elusive goddess – Vernemetum in Willoughby, Nottinghamshire; Nemetostatio in North Tawton, Devon; and Medionemeton near the Antonine Wall in Strathclyde just to name a few. Though She is still wrapped in mystery, Her veneration and fame were, at one time, quite well known throughout the western world.

As the Lady of the Sacred Grove, we may best find Her when we venture out of doors, reconnecting with nature and our ancestors of old. That's the wonderful thing about being in a forest – you are actually *in* it. Not *on* rocks, or *on* the lake or sea, but actually in it, feeling very much a part of it all. The sense of self changes, our perceptions alter slightly when we become a part of something bigger than ourselves. Out of doors, especially in the forest or wood, is where many Druids and Pagans alike go to celebrate, to reconnect and to sing their wild songs.

I've always thought of Nemetona as a relation to the ever elusive goddess Elen. The antlered goddess, Elen is currently undergoing a bit of a resurrection today, with more and more people discovering Her, though physical sources explaining Her and Her attributes are few and far between. Elen is a wild goddess, found deep within the wood. Hidden in the shadows of the trees, she watches you with eyes millennia old. You may catch a brief glimpse of her, and then she is gone, flitting silent as ghost amidst the snowy boughs, disappearing in a heartbeat. She is the heartbeat of the wood, of the wild places, of heathland and moorland. She dances under the moon in star-filled skies, her dance exhilarating and free. And in the blink of an eye she is gone, lost in the mist that slowly curls over the land in eloquent drifts.

Elen seems to have escaped the history books and academia of the human race. She knows this, and it pleases her greatly. You cannot know Her without seeking Her out, in the wild places, in the darkness and in the light, in the heat and in the cold. She is to be experienced, not to be read about. She is Elen of the Ways, of the trackways and paths that cross both nature and the human soul. She is a physical deity – you must put one foot in front of the other if you are ever to know Her. If you are lucky, you can find the ancient pathways she has trod, leaving Her energy behind, enticing you further, deeper into the heart of the wood, where the mysteries lie. Follow the footprints – in the snow, in the mud, in the sand. The cloven hoof of the deer will lead you to Her. They are Her children, they are Her. Like the deer, She is grace and strength, She is trusting and wary, She is capable of great stillness and explosive action. She is curious and wise, and She will beckon you further in if your heart is open.

Even as Elen embodies the wild aspects of our souls, Nemetona is that which is held in deep reverence, in sanctuary. Elen runs wild and free throughout the forest, Nemetona holds that spirit safe within the bounds of her circle, the sacred glade at the heart of the wood. Both goddesses have very little academic and historical knowledge available about them – however, both are very much present here in the British Isles and, indeed, throughout the world.

For me, Nemetona walks gracefully in the heart of the sacred grove, robed in natural linens, white limbs shining in the moonlight, her long dark hair flowing down her back. Elen runs free, flitting between the great trunks of the trees, ghostly as the deer, her limbs browned by the sun and her wild red hair tumbling free about her shoulders. Elen's pathways often lead to Nemetona at the sacred heart of the wood. They often smile to each other, honouring each other and the sanctity of all things.

For those lucky enough to physically have a sacred grove, a forest or woodland to go to on a regular basis, making that commitment to spend time in that very special place can be an excellent way to meet with Nemetona and her wilder sister, Elen.

If you can, find a space where you can go as often as possible, to walk beneath the boughs, to become a part of the forest or wood. If there is a glade within the wood, so much the better – it doesn't have to be big. Sit and meditate there, dance in the moonlight, make an offering to Nemetona in order to establish that deep connection to Her in her sacred grove that words just cannot even begin to describe.

If you don't have access to the physical manifestation of the sacred grove, then you can create one within your soul, the ideal haven for respite, to meet with the goddess and to find yourself in harmony with world. This meditation may also be done within a real forest or wood – indeed, try to do both to see the differences that occur and compare the two.

The Inner Grove Meditation

Find some time when you won't be disturbed and sit comfortably in a quiet place. Light a candle, burn some incense – do whatever makes you feel more comfortable and more in tune with your spirituality. Feel your own nemeton, cast it further to create a sacred circle – it is entirely up to you.

Once you are ready, close your eyes to begin a journey within the mind and soul. Find yourself standing at the forest edge, with two great oak trees framing a darkened entrance to the wood. Behind and extending out to the sides you see a grand variety of trees; yew and pine, holly and ash, all together to create a thick forest that is buzzing and brimming with the songs of the trees and sunshine, wind and rain. You bring your attention back to the gateway, and ask permission to enter the forest from the two oak guardians, stating your intention to meet with Nemetona clearly and firmly within your mind and soul.

A breeze blows at your back, and the oaks seem to wave you forward into the depths of the forest. You take your first steps on the path, feeling the ground firm beneath your feet. Notice the scents that arise, the quality of the light, any movement in the undergrowth. Notice the time of day, the season, what you are wearing.

After a time you come to a thick, almost hedge-like wall of holly. You walk around it, noticing that it forms a circle, deep within the heart of the wood. You return to where you first came across it, and close your eyes, attuning to the deep, dark, rich song of the trees. You feel the spirit of the holly and ask that you may enter the Sacred Grove, once again stating your intention to meet with the Goddess. The holly looks back into your own soul, and seeing your clear intention, slowly parts before you.

You open your eyes and walk forwards into the glade. You look up, and see the trunks of great trees looming over the circling hollies, creating a perfect glade deep within the heart of the forest. You take a deep breath, smelling the air and all its textures, rich with the wild soul of the woodland that surrounds it.

You walk the inner edge of the glade, offering prayers of thanks to the spirits for this time and this place. As you complete the circuit, you walk towards the middle and see a stone set in the centre – it appears to be an altar. You place an offering on the altar, and then sit or stand before it, taking deep breaths and focusing on Her. Once you are ready, you call to Her, to Nemetona. When She is ready, she will come to you.

Pay close attention to what she tells you; ask Her the questions that you hold within your soul. Once you are ready, bow to Her and thank Her for all that she is.

After She has departed, you circle the sacred grove once more, singing softly to the spirits, of thanks and thanksgiving. You arrive once again at the entrance to the sacred grove by the hollies, and with thanks make your way through. Retracing your path through the wood, you eventually come back to the oak guardians. Holding your arms above your head, you offer them thanks, and walk beneath their sheltering arms. Once outside the forest, you turn and bow, your spirit honouring its spirit. You may even see Elen smiling beneath the shadowy boughs.

You become aware of yourself once again, in meditation. When you are ready, open your eyes and fully return to this time and space. Thank the goddess for what you have learned, and offer Her something in this physical world. Share some food and drink with those of the wild around you, to leave outside if possible for those little souls to partake in. Know that you are honoured, by honouring Her in her sacred grove.

Chapter Four

The Lady of Sanctuary

Sanctuary – it is such a beautiful word. Derived from the Latin *sanctus*, meaning holy or hallowed, and the suffix *ary*, meaning connected with, it offers a vision of a sacred place. Most people in today's society now think of sanctuary as a refuge, most often for birds or other wildlife. Yet it is so much more than that – it is a place where all are not only protected, but where all can be nurtured, to grow and find the freedom that we need to live our lives in true expression of our soul song. It is also about providing this for others, and learning about the nature of sanctuary in order to work better with it for the benefit of everyone and everything.

In the conventional sense, a sanctuary is a hallowed space, made holy usually by human hands. However, Druids can normally find these places in the wildest of places, where no human hands have ever been, honouring the spirits of place that created this sanctuary. As an animist, I think that the creation of a sanctuary is not solely a human expression of divine inspiration, or awen. I believe that the multitudes of other beings and souls on this planet can do exactly the same. The elephant graveyards, for example, are a beautiful expression of another species' creation of hallowed ground. (The jury is still out on whether this is true or not; however, it strikes chords of truth within my own soul.) There is a Native American saying, that birds create their nests in circles, for their religion is the same as ours...

In the human sense, most often we think of sanctuary in buildings, such as churches and other religious edifices. Many people will be familiar with a story of someone – a fugitive from justice – seeking sanctuary, pounding on the doors of the church or monastery, calling "Sanctuary! Sanctuary!" and being let in, thereby coming under the law of the religious order and thus exempt from secular justice.

Yet to many Pagans sanctuary exists in a wide variety of places, recognised or not by the Abrahamic faiths and their religious structures. They may be in stone circles on windswept moors, created by our Neolithic ancestors. They may be in a room set aside in our house for meditation, for peace and sanctuary. It may be a graveyard in a city cemetery, or a shrine on top of a mountain. What is required is the ability to recognise a place as offering sanctuary. We must *look* for Nemetona.

I hate working in the city. The noise, the pollution and the masses of humanity are a constant barrage against my senses. I am not built for city living. There is no space to relax, my nemeton constantly coming into contact with others, jostling on busy city streets. I feel as if I cannot let my guard down, there is no safe space to do so.

On my lunch break, I take the elevator down twenty-three storeys to ground level, and walk out into the hot, humid haze of August in Montreal. People are eating their lunches in the paved courtyard where skyscrapers converge, amidst fountains and full sun. I walk through the courtyard, seeking a quieter space that I recently found.

Two blocks down and around the corner stands the church. As a Pagan Druid I smile at the irony as I enter through the doors, saying a prayer of thanksgiving as I enter. The air inside is cool, and the silence wraps around me like a comforting hug. Yet the ceiling is still too high, and there are several people walking around, lighting candles or speaking in very hushed voices.

Making my way to the other side of the church, I go to the little wooden chapel dedicated to Mary. In here, it is always empty. I take a spot on one of the pews and allow my soul to relax, looking at the statue of Mary and seeing within her open arms my Lady Nemetona, welcoming me into her embrace. "Sit, stay awhile, be refreshed," she seems to say. I smile and close my eyes, my nemeton relaxing from its tight constrictive circles, layer upon layer in this urban sprawl, and I smell the wax of the candles and incense. In this space I am held, for nearly an hour, finding the space to simply be.

It does not matter if you are a part of a particular faith or not – in these sacred, hallowed spaces all are welcome. Perhaps in the case of some, it is with the ulterior motive that you may change your mind and your religious persuasion, but really what matters is the offering of a safe place. This may or may not be for religious reasons – there are so many reasons for seeking sanctuary.

In the UK at the time of writing, a certain political party wants to put a five-year freeze on immigrants to British shores for various reasons, without any amnesty for illegal immigrants, whatever their reasons (refugee status included). To me this is like a church or monastery shutting its doors on the person seeking sanctuary like in the previous example. This avails nothing – it is dishonourable to say the least, considering that the UK is an island that has been made up of immigrants for thousands of years.

Some towns and cities are going in the opposite direction. On Wednesday 31st October 2012, Ipswich Borough Council passed a resolution of support towards Ipswich becoming a "Town of Sanctuary". From its website, Ipswich Town of Sanctuary states:

> Ipswich Town of Sanctuary is part of the national movement "City of Sanctuary". The aim of the movement is for local groups to work to build coalitions of organisations from all sectors (faith groups, voluntary, business, education, etc) which make a public commitment to welcome and include Refugees and people seeking sanctuary in their usual activities.

This is a beautiful statement that honours the concept of sanctuary in all things, especially for those human beings who so need it in their lives – those who are avoiding persecution or danger. At the time of writing, there are about twenty other cities and towns across the nation doing the same. As a devotee of Nemetona, this is truly inspiring for me!

These notions of sanctuary, the whole concept around it, is not external to us but can also permeate into our own homes. We can have a room set aside specifically called the Sanctuary Room, if we are lucky enough to have the space. Bedrooms are also good places for Sanctuary Rooms, especially if you share yours with someone else, whether it be a partner, relative or even your pet.

To have a dedicated, welcoming space set aside where everyone can simply be, can only be healthy. In these spaces, we may gather together to meditate as a family, simply sitting and breathing together. My husband and I gather together with the cats in the evenings in the conservatory – it is a special place, where silence reigns, and we simply sit together, enjoying each other's presence. It is not a place for heated debates and discussions. It is a quiet space, a welcoming space (in fact, I try to create that in the whole house). It is a gathering point where people and souls meet each other respectfully, simply enjoying the moment. This could also be at the dinner table, or in your lover's arms before you fall asleep – the possibilities are endless.

We create sanctuaries and havens for other species as well, if we can. A place where they are protected from harm, where their soul song can sing free. Bird sanctuaries are popular places, as are nature reserves. We can create that in our own backyards if we are able, leaving patches to grow wild, having ponds and putting food out for the birds in the hungry seasons. It is a place of the least possible interference with the natural flow and cycle of the little brothers and sisters that we share this planet with, from the nettle to the beetle, the dragonflies to the badgers. These places become hallowed by the energy of these creatures, becoming filled with their intentions, their songs and their lives. We can, inspired by Nemetona, keep these places for them safe and protected.

Spend some time in your local patch looking for these external places of sanctuary. Offer your time and energy to a place of sanctuary, such as at a women's shelter, or a shelter for the homeless, or an animal sanctuary. Once we find the gift of sanctuary all around us, we will want to offer it to others as well.

We have seen in a previous chapter the Inner Grove Meditation. As well as external, physical manifestations of sanctuary, there are also inner sanctuaries that we can create, filled with the blessing and the power of Nemetona – a space where we can feel safe, a place where transformation, healing, integration and all manner of things can take place. Now what I would like to suggest below is not so much an inner ritual area like the Inner Grove, but another safe place to use as a "base" for inner journeying – I like to think of it as my Inner Hut.

Creating inner worlds is not only great fun, but a great way to express and confront issues that we physically may not be able to, or which may not be appropriate to do. Several of my teachers have used the idea of an inner safe place which we can use as a starting point, and from there travel out into the wider realms of the mind, exploring what we need to explore. We may have fantastical adventures in our inner worlds, or enjoy the more mundane things within them that we may not have the time to do in our physical world. The Inner Hut provides the starting point, the sanctuary.

My Inner Hut is a place that I can go to in meditation, when I am called to journey, perhaps, or when I feel I need to really take a good look at something that is troubling me in my life, or when I simply need to be refreshed by the blessings that particular sanctuary provides. If an answer isn't available in the so-called mundane world, one may be found in the inner world.

My Inner Hut is a simple, single-room dwelling deep within the heart of an ancient forest, close to a slow-moving river that winds its way through the trees and out into the wider world beyond. It is a simple wattle and daub hut, with a thatched roof that occasionally needs repair and a dirt floor. Inside there is a table in the centre, with two benches on either side, a bed along one wall and a chest at the foot of the bed. There is a much-used hearth on the back wall, and a good stack of firewood both inside and outside the hut. There is also a chair pulled up near the hearth, and a large wooden basin on a separate smaller table under the window. Herbs are hung to dry from the ceiling, and my staff leans in the corner by the door.

This hut is my safe space and my starting point for any adventures that I may wish to undertake in the inner realms. Sometimes it is simply enough to just spend some time in the hut, or around it, looking at the herbs growing nearby, sitting by the river's edge and watching the water flow past. If there is an issue to deal with, I can either deal with it in this safe space, or venture further out into the woods to find just what it is that needs to be taken care of, knowing that I always have this safe haven, this little sanctuary to return to should it be needed.

Below is a little journey meditation that you can use to find your Inner Hut, and from there explore the depths of the mind and specific issues, knowing that you have an inner sanctuary to return to, should it be required.

Inner Hut Meditation

Spend some time in your meditation space, simply breathing, relaxing into the present moment. Do not think of anything in particular – if thoughts do arise, then simply notice them and then bring your focus back to the present moment and your breathing. Sit like this for five or ten minutes.

Now it is time to begin your journey to your Inner Hut. Close your eyes, and in your mind's eye, allow the area around you to slowly melt away, to be replaced with a landscape of your choice – something that you feel comfortable in, that sings to your very soul. Take a few deep breaths, and focus on the new environment. Look around in front of you, noticing everything that you can. Then, turn around, and see your Inner Hut, waiting for you, the door open. What does it look like? What is it made of? How does it sit within the landscape?

You walk towards the open door, and at the doorway pause for a moment, uttering a prayer to Nemetona. You then enter into the hut, taking a deep breath. What does it smell like? Looking around you, what do you see? The hut is filled with things that have meaning to you and your life – practical things and decoration alike. The hut is yours and yours alone, a place where you can simply be, without worry, without fear.

Take a moment to really explore your hut. Feel any objects, sit on any furniture, observe what there is and what there isn't in this place. Do anything that might make you feel even more at home within it – make a cup of tea, light the fire, prepare some food. When you have thoroughly explored the inside of the structure, touching all the walls and furniture, seeing every nook and cranny, listening to the sounds around you, then step outside once more.

Around you is your landscape, that place that you have decided to call home away from home. Look around, knowing that within that landscape are a myriad possibilities for you to explore. You may want to rush out straight away from this safe haven and fight a dragon, or talk to the elves, or search for that sacred herb that might help you in your dilemma. But for now, simply stay a while, getting to know your sanctuary first. Only then, when we are truly aware of our haven and its boundaries, can we venture forth with the knowledge that we are able to return; we can seek the time and space that we need for whatever reason. Time spent being within that inner landscape, to establish this sanctuary, is reason enough. Sit within your Inner Hut, while the rain or wind howls outside. Sit outside, while the sun shines down. Sing to the land around your place, getting to know it and allowing it to know you. Honour this landscape and the goddess, and you will be rewarded for many years to come with a place of inner sanctuary.

Once you are ready to leave, take a few deep breaths and

allow the landscape around you to melt away, slowly revealing the landscape that you are currently in – the physical world. Breathe here for a few moments, fully returning to yourself and your environment. Make an offering, if you can, to the goddess for whatever has taken place.

Chapter Five

Lady of Ritual

Ritual – the word rolls off the tongue. It evokes images of moonlight and standing stones, or incense and flower-filled temple rooms, women and men gathered under the stars or the light of day to celebrate an aspect of life, death and rebirth.

Ritual is as simple or complex as we allow it to be. We can follow a set liturgy, or we can create our own path. Within Paganism, both are equally acceptable. As Modern Paganism is, technically, a newly rebirthed religion the question of authenticity with regards to validity is moot – someone, somewhere along the line, whether it was sixty years ago, six-hundred years ago or sixty-thousand years ago, made it up at some point. That has no bearing on its validity.

When we create ritual, we are taking a moment, taking time out, to celebrate or honour a specific moment in time. It may be as simple as saying a prayer of thanks at sunrise or sunset, or it may be a full blown affair held within a stone circle, with twenty or more participants, having rehearsed their roles and re-enacting a mythic drama. Whatever ritual you choose to perform, establishing a relationship with Nemetona can be a rich and rewarding experience to lend to these sacred acts.

Nemetona is Lady of the Sacred Grove, where it is believed that ritual occurred in past history. The ritual itself is just as important as the setting. It must speak to us, must sing to our soul, otherwise, what is the point?

As the Lady of Holding, of guarding and watching over our sacred space, our created sanctuaries, Nemetona is also a Lady of Ritual, integral to it if we so desire. She moves in circles and in cycles, and therefore when we hold a ritual circle, we can invoke her easily within that sacred place. She is all that is within the sacred circle, and also all that is without. Like a vase, the vase is not only the boundaries of its own edges, but also the emptiness within that allows it to be a vase as well as the space outside that allows its form to be.

We can call upon Nemetona in ritual, to protect our sacred circle, to bless it, or simply to witness what it is that we are doing within that space (or all three). She can be called upon before a ritual to help define its intent and purpose. She is the Lady of Holding, and within her embrace we are free to be and do as we wish. Within the sacred ritual circle, she enables change and growth, safety and security where we might otherwise feel it lacking.

Within the ritual circle is a space where we can grow, where we can make associations and develop our spirituality to its true potential. Within the sacred circle, we overlay it with our associations in ritual such as the elements, our spirit guides, ancestors, gods and goddesses and more. By finding out where these "fit" in the sacred ritual circle, held within the arms of Nemetona we come to truly understand ourselves, and the greater world at large.

I was taught to physically draw out the circle and explore it as an exercise in learning more about my own sacred circle. I chose an old cotton bed sheet that was no longer being used, and using fabric paints created the sacred circle that I previously only saw in my head. I made it big enough so that I could physically sit or stand within it. I divided it up into four quarters, and associated each quarter with a colour, turning my circle into spiritual artwork. I wrote the names of the seasonal celebrations around the edges of the circle where they corresponded for me, and the seasons themselves. I found embroidered appliqué animals, and sewed them into the spaces where I thought they belonged. I made that sacred circle to reflect my own soul, and all the associations that I held with that space that Nemetona guards, holds and enfolds.

Sitting upon that circle, I could then explore more fully other aspects of my life, to see where they fit in the circle. I looked at each member of my family, and where they were in the circle – were they in the right place? If not, what could I do to get them to where they would fit better? I found hidden things that I had not noticed were there. Using that technique, I undertook several months of seeing how pieces of the puzzle fit – it was a brilliant exercise in finding one's own sacred circle, deep within one's own nemeton and held by the goddess Herself. There, we are free to explore ourselves fully, for She is that which holds, embraces and acts as witness to our ritual.

Ritual for me is now multi-faceted, after doing that exercise and exploration. The sacred circle has taken on so many new meanings for me, enriching it with all the associations that I have come to know over my life and through my relationship with Her.

Creating Your Own Physical Sacred Circle

Using the above ideas, try to create your own physical sacred circle. You can use fabric and paints like I did, or draw a circle in chalk upon the ground, or the floorboards of your home. You can delineate the edges with flowers, their colours and placement being meaningful to you and your personal associations. You can simply draw it on a piece of paper. Delve deeply into these associations – what colour is north in your circle? What does east sound like? What animal resides in the south? What does west taste like? Where would your father and mother fit in this circle? Where would your gods, your ancestors?

This exercise can either be created physically, as above, with paints and designs, or entirely explored within the mind. It is easiest to at least have a physical representation of a circle in which to sit, so that you can look around both in your mind's eye and also with your own eyes if necessary. Plus, it's fun to get creative and messy! With a physical representation that you can roll up and take with you, you can explore these things deep in the woods, or in your meditation room, or your hotel room even!

Once you are familiar with your sacred circle, you can leave the physical representation behind (though it is helpful to go back to it every now and then, to discover where things are, if they have moved, where new things fit). All these associations you can carry within your mind, and so imprint them upon your circle when casting, no matter where you are. The ritual circle will become a part of yourself, not merely a representation of who and what you are, but an extension of yourself that you can use for transformation and growth.

Casting Your Own Sacred Circle

How, you may ask, does one go about casting the ritual/sacred circle, after understanding it physically? This can be difficult for some, for it requires the essential tool of visualisation, together with power from within to make that sacred space.

There are as many different methods of casting the circle as there are people who are casting. Each and every method is equally valid if it works for the individual, as long as there is no harm done to oneself or others in the process. Here is how I cast a circle for ceremonial purposes (simpler circles are cast at other times) – you may come to find your own way, or already have an understanding of how you can do so yourself, to be layered with a newfound understanding of the Lady of Ritual. For group gatherings, a "looser" circle may be cast, to enable the blending of others' nemetons to create sacred space and also allow the energy to flow freely throughout the ritual to others who may either be participating or simply witnessing.

Standing facing north, hold out both arms at your sides, palms facing north. Raise both arms slowly overhead, gathering the energy of the land, sea and sky. Once both hands are overhead, bring them together to "seal" that connection with the energy, and then lower your hands in prayer position down past your face and coming to rest above your heart. Know that you are centred, with the energy of the world both within you and outside of you, ever-flowing. Call to Nemetona to guide you, to aid you, to help hold and create this sacred space.

Next, still facing north, take your dominant hand (right hand if you are right-handed, left hand if you are left-handed) and push the energy out from your centre that you have gathered within. Next, walk the circle's edge. Some say that you should walk clockwise, the direction of the sun, but I've always found this a little odd, as it is the earth that spins, and therefore walking counter-clockwise is walking in the direction of the spinning earth (if you are looking down from the North Pole to the South Pole, reverse for South Pole to North Pole). It also depends on the people participating in the ritual – if they prefer the circle be walked clockwise, then I will adjust to suit their needs. Again, to each their own – as long as it harms none, as the famous Wiccan Rede states, which many Pagans adhere to.

However you walk the circle, push the energy out of your palm, creating a waist-high line of energy. I visualise this as a blue-white line of energy – you can choose the colour that best represents your own soul or need. When you have returned to the start point, close off the energy from your palm when it touches the edge of the circle from where you started. Then, as before, slowly raise your arms overhead, raising the energy coming into prayer position, lowering before your face. When your hands are held at chest level, expand the line that you created, upwards and downwards, to turn your circle now into a sphere. Sweep it around, making it larger if necessary. You can lower the centre line through your visualisation down until it touches the earth, creating a half sphere above the earth and a half sphere below the earth. Take a moment, feeling the circle/sphere that you have created, honouring Nemetona as you do so. Feel the associations that you have come to learn about your circle, seeing them there, where they fit, where they guide and where they guard, where they inspire and where they may hide. Know that this circle is an aspect of your soul.

I then consecrate the circle with incense, to represent the elements of air, fire and earth, and then I consecrate with water. I begin at the north edge and walk the circle round again, with a feather and censer for incense, then scattering drops of water with my fingers on the third turn with a bowl of water. After I have returned to where I started, the circle will have been walked three times.

The elements may now be invoked, the ancestors honoured and the deities called to, if you so wish. The statement of intention is spoken, and the ritual act then occurs.

Taking down the sacred circle is simply a reverse of the casting – draw the energy back into yourself and walk in the reverse direction to casting. Then, when back at the north release the energy back into the land, sea and sky by reversing the hand gestures – bring your hands together at heart level and then raise them past your face, opening outwards and down to release.

By coming to know and understand yourself better, through your sacred circle, you also come closer to Nemetona herself. Within the sacred circle of ritual we can come closer to Her, in perfect love and perfect trust.

Chapter Six

The Lady of Everything and Nothing

Within Nemetona's embrace, we find that sacred space where we are held, nurtured, guarded. In that space, we are allowed to change, to create change both within ourselves and, through changing ourselves, our world as well. We can create a time out of time, a space out of space, within which to find that sanctuary to allow our souls to sing free. When we are free, anything is possible.

Nemetona is not just a Lady of the Sacred Circle – she is also a Lady of the Sacred Cycle. Within her circles and groves we see the reflection of the whole world. In each circle that we cast, within each grove that we dance, is a microcosm of the world, the universe. We fill it with our known associations, making it easier to understand our place. And yet the boundary of the circle is not where She ends. For She is both inside and outside the circle – She is all that lies within and all that lies without. Like the vase mentioned earlier, She is not just the form itself, but the empty spaces both within and without that make it what it is.

When we relax into Nemetona's arms, we allow ourselves to float free. We can, if we so wish, give ourselves over to Her embrace, for however short a time, in order to feel that freedom that is otherwise hard to attain within the physical body. The universe is such a vast thing – we have difficulty connecting with such a huge concept. By letting go of our sense of self, by releasing into Her embrace, we can safely go there for a time, returning to our selves when we have sated our desire to know what it is we wish to know, to experience that which cannot normally be experienced.

Sometimes we have to lose ourselves in order to find ourselves.

That immersion into the entirety of being is what many Druids and other Pagans crave. To be at one with existence, to truly experience life. It is both terrifying and inviting at the same time. We feel we must hold on to our sense of self, otherwise we face oblivion.

Who am I? Philosophers, religions, spiritualities and people all over the world have asked themselves this question – is there truly a self at all?

The Materialists would say that there is no self at all – that there is no consciousness, that we are simply matter and energy and the result of material interactions. Descartes stated: "I think therefore I am", to which the Materialists refuted Descartes dualism of a separate mind and body, ridiculing it as "ghost in the machine". Zen and Buddhism talks about a True Self that can only be realised by dropping all ideas of the self and achieving a pure state of being in the moment, a state of total selflessness in every sense of the word.

Nietzsche stated that: "We have never sought ourselves, how could it happen that we should ever find ourselves?" He believed that we are a result of our experiences and actions, but that there still was a Self, a consciousness. In order to be complete, Nietzsche said that we must learn acceptance – to accept everything we have ever done. I find this fascinating, because how many times have we done things during our lives, stating that we were out of our minds, or did something "that was not me at all" – stepping outside of the core idea of what we are? This acceptance, instead of avoidance, is key to the deeper understanding of the self, in my opinion. Acceptance doesn't mean liking everything that we may have done in the past, nor does it define us in the present moment, but what it does allow is a total non-judgemental overview of the self, and in doing so, a deep awareness that we might not achieve by avoidance of the subject. By obtaining that deeper awareness, we are also more able to let it go into Nemetona's embrace, for however long or short a period we desire.

Before Nietzche, Kierkegaard put forward the notion of choosing to be self-aware. We are homo sapiens, after all – in fact, I believe the proper term for our species is homo sapiens sapiens – the beings that are aware that they are aware. Kierkegaard stated that when we choose to be self-aware, we are both aware of our self and, at the same time, aware that we are aware of our self. Observing the observer who is observing. Yet we choose not to observe, because we often don't like what we see or experience, either in the past, present or future.

This is all fascinating. And also requires some very deep thinking. There is a theory of No Self from Zen Buddhism, which is a paradigm of course, as is much in Zen. The No Self is also the True Self. It states that our real self is in existence, always, and always has been. It is pure, and shining free – we only distract ourselves from it to such an extent that we never see it. Zen states that we are already complete, already whole, already perfect.

This is pretty simple to understand, and it makes sense. The difficulties, the suffering in our lives detract us from spending time in the pure moment, in which the True Self resides. We suffer because we want things to be different, because we desire things, people, etc – and are not happy with the present moment as it is. If we are happy and accepting of the present moment as it is, without judgement of good or bad, or any attachment to it at all, then we can rediscover this True Self. By letting go of all notions of the Self, we return to the core, essentially.

In Zen Buddhism, the term *mu* can mean a multitude of things – it essentially, and paradoxically, means "nothing". It can be termed as "no self", "no ego", "no holiness" and "imperma-nence". It is the transcending of all things, the enlightenment experience, the complete and utter letting go of affirmations and negations. It is an answer to some Zen koans (questions asked to break apart the mind and let in a new way of understanding). Zen master Keido Fukishima, like Kierkegaard, promotes the self-inquiry into our own being and mind, to be aware that we are being aware. In Zen, this has the goalless goal of letting go – once we have found our mind, we lose it (not in an insane way, I might add) and in the losing, in the understanding of the impermanence of all things, including the mind and the self, we rediscover the True Self. Keido Fukushima says, "Zen teaches us how to live by inquiring into and clarifying ourselves. This self-questioning is well suited to our contemporary ways of thinking. Rather than seeking salvation through an "other" or through grace, we achieve it on our own."

Fukushima delves further into this idea, stating:

> The experience of mu may at first glance seem purely negative or passive, but it is not so at all. Being mu, or empty of self, allows one to actively take in whatever comes. Our world today and all in it are separated into dualistic distinctions of good and evil, birth and death, gain and loss, self and other, and so on. By being mu, not only does one's self-centeredness disappear – the conflicts that arise with others dissolve as well. Here is a simple example: When we look at a mountain, we tend to observe it as an object. But if we are mu, we no longer see the mountain as an object; we identify with it; we are the mountain itself. This transcendence of duality may sound like some psychic ability or spiritual power someone possesses. But that is not true. Rather, it is simply and naturally a case of being free, creative, and fresh. We become human beings full of boundless love and compassion. (See bibliography for more on Fukishima.)

This rejects the Dualists' (such as Descartes') theories and instead breaks down all barriers, which is both liberating and frightening at the same time. There is no *Us and Them*, no *Self and the Other* – if we truly let go of all attachment we become one with everything. Are we willing to do that, or are we too attached to our sense of self to experience that? Can we truly dissolve into everything?

It comes in small flashes, in glimpses, held within Nemetona's embrace. The world, wrapped up in an apple, in a drop of rain, in the flight of a hawk. Barriers are dropped, ego and self have fallen away, and we see the multitudes of the universe.

This is passing through the Gateless Gate – I've also heard it called the groundless ground. In realising the impermanence of everything, including the Self, we have a platform from which to jump from into real living, where every moment counts and is never the same. The Self changes from moment to moment.

This is hard, for we have spent our whole lives creating this sense of self, this timeless sense of self that we think defines us. Starting with acceptance, and then moving on, letting go, without attachment, is crucial. Maybe then the True Self will shine again, for longer and longer moments, ever shifting, ever changing, always truthful. However, as Freud said, "It's just a theory."

The entirety of the world can be contained within a single drop of dew on a flower petal in the light of the dawn. We can look up into the night sky and see just how vast our world really is. We can dance in the light of the fire, casting its sacred circle of light in the grove. We can sit together in a circle and take turns really speaking and listening to each other, without judgement and with compassion. In these things we can be inspired by this goddess, learning and growing, held within Her sanctuary. She is everything that ever existed; She is the dark vastness of nothing. Dance with Her.

Within the circle's firelight, I shed my clothing, the trees still and silent in the hushed, warm summer night air. I raise my arms with a smile, and welcome My Lady. She is always with me and without me, but sometimes I forget. I honour Her with all that I am, and I begin to move, my body swaying slightly with the music in my heart. I start to dance the circle round, an ecstatic dance of joy and celebration of My Lady. Within this dance I weave the stories of my life, and I see the stories of others there too. I see the myriad worlds, possibilities, and I dance, ever quicker, calling out to Her. Before I know it She is there, watching me, a faint smile upon her lips. She glides over to me and takes my hands, and the world spins in dizzying circles as I see the ages of the world flash by, galaxies rotating in their spiral dances. I let myself go fully into Her, and in that vast darkness there is everything and nothing. I float for a time in that space, without any sense of who I am, unafraid. I let go. After a time, the darkness slowly recedes, and the world comes back into my vision, the firelight lower now, the cries of the owl in the branches overhead. I see Her standing at the circle's edge, still smiling faintly, and I smile back.

Appendices

Appendix I

Nemetona Through the Eyes of Others

Here I wished to include others' visions of this goddess and what she represents, to expand upon my own view of Her. As there is so little that is actually known of Her, hearing how others connect with Her can be deeply inspiring.

Who Nemetona is to Me

by Ellen Evert Hopman

Nemetona is one of my favourite goddesses. I have always been a human companion to cats and my cats have all had god or goddess names. This past January I lost my soul cat, Nemetona, a beautiful smoky grey and orange tortoiseshell cat, who lent her graceful presence to my life for thirteen years. Her Spirit has now melted into the wilderness, her bones lie beneath a giant oak behind the house.

I meet Nemetona the goddess most vividly when I take walks in the wild, usually by myself and sometimes with a cat by my side. For me she is the unseen but deeply felt Spirit of Nature. I may wander for hours before I meet Her. At some point She is simply there. I know this because there is a subtle shift in the atmosphere. The light changes and sight wavers. Perhaps the birds stop singing for no apparent reason or the wind stills.

I like to stop and sit at that time, lowering my gaze through half opened eyes, to meditate under the trees. At such times my deepest questions will be answered and I always rise refreshed and ready to resume my tasks and projects.

Many years ago I visited the Maniwaki Native American reservation in Canada, to attend the yearly four-day peace gathering held by Grandfather Commanda. Asleep in my tent, I heard a voice; a woman was making a speech about respect. In my dream she was telling me and others that the essence of what we had to do was to respect the herbs and trees and not cut them down. She said we had to respect the waters and not pollute them. We had to respect the fire and the air and earth and stop clogging them with waste, and that we needed to be kind to the animals and also respect the sacred human beings. We had to live that way in this world.

The next day I attended a workshop given by Grandmother Lillian and I was astounded to hear the exact same words coming out of her mouth, the words that I had heard spoken in my dream.

This book, *Dancing with Nemetona* breathes the same message. When we can learn to feel the goddess who protects the sacred Grove, and when we realise that She is the Spirit within all things, we will be on our way to finding true peace in this world. We will become the true protectors of the Earth and Her creatures.

Ellen Evert Hopman is the author of the novels Priestess of the Forest – A Druid Journey, The Druid Isle, Priestess of the Fire Temple – A Druid's Tale and other books about sacred trees and herbal medicine. www.elleneverthopman.com.

Nemetona

by Maria Ede-Weaving

Nemetona's essence resides in the sacred space of our hearts; her presence shimmering in those special places where the sanctuary of our being widens to inhabit the sacredness of the earth. I feel her when I engage with the earth in an intimate way. Through her, I celebrate not only the beauty of the sacred circle but also the holy grove of my own heart and being. She is the sacred relationship that I strive to build with my environment and the many beings that inhabit it; she is the sacred relationship I strive to build with myself.

She is not just a goddess of the grove; she wears the changing colours of place and time. The sacred circle is a richly layered mandala of change, the spiralling cycles that bring us movement and transformation, not only in the physical world of the seasons but also in the cyclical natures of our emotions, minds, bodies and souls. Nemetona nurtures and supports that transformation, holding us in her peace, opening us to her wisdom that the changes might bring healing and flow to our lives. I associate her with the butterfly – symbol of the soul's journey of freedom, movement and joy. Like her, butterflies encourage us to recognise the quality of each season and its impact upon us; the letting go, the stasis, the waiting, the awakening, the blossoming, the fruiting – within Nemetona's loving arms we can engage more fully with each, never losing sight of the eternal soul within.

Nemetona's connection to trees links her to the breath of life. Both are intimately interwoven with the drawing in of inspiration and the outward expression of our own unique voice and ability to create. There is a strong tradition in Druidry between the sacred and our ability to create. When we breathe the sacred into our being – nourishing our cells and souls – we also feed our creativity, opening the channels for inspiration and, in doing so, transforming our creativity into an act of worship. There is an exchange that takes place – a breathing in of the one and an outpouring of the other – setting up a circuit as vital as the continuous exchange between the carbon dioxide and oxygen that we and the trees depend upon for life.

Nemetona has taught me that the inhalation and exhalation of the breath of life – the acknowledgement of this as a sacred act – is the core of my inspiration. Sitting quietly, reaching for my still centre, letting her flood my heart, I feel that precious and true sense of belonging, peace and joy – I am fit to burst with it. Isn't this why the bird sings? When we give our creativity to the world – responsibly and with love – we become a dawn chorus, a full throated celebration of the creative force of life that is reborn within us daily.

Maria Ede-Weaving writes A Druid Thurible Blog.

Walking the Edges

by Nimue Brown

I've never understood how some Pagans seem comfortable walking into the middle of a space and just getting on with it. However, in many ritual spaces I've found a shortage of time or opportunity to do anything other than get in circle. What I prefer to do, when alone, is walk the edges first. Maybe once, maybe more than once depending on how well I know the space. Time to recognise the borders, and get a sense of the energy of it. I'll go round the outside of stone circles, ritual spaces, around barrows and so forth. It gives me time to become aware, to see the space from all directions and get a sense of how it sits in a landscape. Only then do I feel wholly easy about moving into the middle.

Walking, for me, is how I do most of my private Druidry. There are echoes of beating the bounds, an old tradition of marking the edges of parishes, in this urge to go around. I like to know the shape of a space, the point at which it becomes somewhere else. "Hail spirits of place" makes a lot more sense if you know where the place is, and where it ends.

Boundaries matter to me, and I hold my own carefully. I don't like it when people bound into my space uninvited and put hands on me. Therefore I treat ritual spaces with the same care I like to be shown. That begins with not assuming I have a right to be there, or a right to wade in and take what I want. It requires having a bit more time and not treating space as a commodity to be used. It is a nonsense to me to address spirits of place in a spiritual way whilst treating place like another thing that exists only for our benefit.

Nimue Brown is the author of assorted Druidry books and works of fiction. She is also a regular blogger at www.druidlife.wordpress.com.

Nemetona is Water

by Suvi

Nemetona is the Goddess of Sacred Space; to me all is sacred, so everything and everyone is part Nemetona; fifty-five per cent to seventy-eight per cent in fact, dependent on gender, age and build: Nemetona is water!

Her sacredness is her continuous cycle; life-giving and affirming if respected, life-threatening and ending if not. Worked with, but never tamed, with the illusion of civilisation laid bare by lack of or too much rain.

Icecaps are her body; evaporation and precipitation, her breathing; clouds, her moods; springs and streams, her veins; rivers, her arteries; the oceans, her heart and the tides its beat.

Physically she is nature's metabolism. Hampered she will stunt growth not only environmentally, but politically, socially and economically and for the individual their health and wellbeing.

A liquid crystal and very old, the rain molecules (perfect spheres without gravity) falling today are up to 3,000 years old; water stored in underground caves and coming to the surface as springs can be over 10,000 years old, to flow downstream and into all of our futures. Little wonder then that our human understanding of water is also spiritual. As Druids we yearn for balance; it is no surprise that we are drawn to lush water-infused environments as spiritual oases. Nemetona here is protective and nurturing in their personal development, allowing the individual the comfort to go with the flow and not fight the current.

So how do we work with Nemetona in the 21st century? We do not waste water; we only use what we need. We do not pollute water through littering and we complain if sewerage is tipped into water courses. We join campaigns and petitions to halt building on flood plains and pollution by industries and, most importantly, we work towards an end to water poverty, as equality in access to water will lead through Nemetona's metabolism to a balanced global peaceful society. Making water a commodity is the greatest crime of our age. It is not to go unchallenged on our watch and not continue in our name.

Suvi is an Animist Druid in Leeds, United Kingdom.

Appendix II

Who Were the Druids?

To look at Druid history we must look to the history of the Celts, who they were and where they came from. There is a growing theory that the Celts had Indo-European roots dating back to around 4,000 BCE and migrated across Europe to finally settle in France, Britain and Ireland. Traces of Celtic culture and history can be found all throughout Europe.

The large Celtic migration theory holds that the Celts, after arriving in Britain, came across the native British tribes and either war or intermarriage ensued. There is another theory, however, that proposes the native British tribes grew into bigger and more socially complex societies, into which some Continental Celts settled and from which the Celtic cultural and religious ideas spread into Europe, rather than the other way around. This theory would hold that Druidry is the native religion of Britain. Both theories are interesting and as yet remain to be proven; however, the leaning is still towards larger migrations or invasions into Britain.

It is difficult to interpret Druid history, as indeed like most historical accounts, their story was written usually by the winners or those hostile to the Celts in any sort of conflict. The ancient Celtic peoples followed an oral tradition, and as such there are no written records in their own voices. Classical sources have written about the Celts, describing them as barbaric, or if feeling more generous, noble savages. They write of a hierarchy based upon the tribe's standing in war – essentially the strongest arm ruled the tribe and/or many other tribes. They also describe women warriors as equally fierce as their male counterparts.

The Druids are commonly believed to the priestly caste of the Celts, whose service was to the Gods and to their people. The perception is that they held considerable sway in the sociological foundations of Celtic life, being the law-makers and king-makers. The Druids and indeed the Celts abided largely by the concept of giving their word – once given it was criminal and exceedingly distasteful to rescind. This links in with reputation – what was said of a person was of great import in Celtic society. A person's reputation was linked to their standing in society, where being strong, generous, brave, wise and just was the ideal.

The Druids were said to gather in "sacred groves"; Druidry today, perhaps more than any other strand of Paganism in the wide weave of spiritual traditions, takes the environment into consideration on so many levels. Druidry – most commonly believed to be from the old Irish words dru and wid meaning "oak knower", or even the Proto-European deru and weid "oak-seeker" – acknowledges this communion with nature in the very roots (pardon the pun) of the word. It is often only within the language of Druidry that we hear of the goddess Nemetona, or the word nemeton, though it is not exclusive to Druidry, but simply more popular.

For a more in depth look at the Druids, please see Ronald Hutton's *Blood and Mistletoe: The History of the Druids in Britain.*

Appendix III

Nemetona and the Micro-Retreat

We all need a place to retreat to, every now and then. A place to withdraw, to regroup, to reharness our energy and so to come back out into the world with renewed energy. Everyone is familiar with the summer holiday, or some time off in the bleak of midwinter. These are chances to lay aside the worries of work and to get back in touch with yourself, your family, and what really matters. However, what if we managed to do that each and every day? Mini or micro-breaks, at least once a day, to reconnect those threads of the weave that we have dropped, to re-establish relationships and to fully honour the time that we are alive...

Every day is a chance to stop, to enter into ritual, to take a step back and simply savour the moment. We can become so out of tune with our own bodies; is it any wonder that other people often baffle us? By understanding ourselves, we can better understand others and so work to help others in a more positive, productive way.

So we create the micro-retreat. We can do this in honour of Nemetona, the goddess of the Sacred Grove, Lady of Ritual and Sanctuary. Once a day, we stop, and take a moment to watch the moon, or sit on a cushion and meditate, to attune to our sense of self or let go of that sense of self to gain full immersion in the present moment. When we find that centre point, that sense of self, we can then let it go, and seek out the deeper connections that can be found when the self is released. We are all living on this planet together and by dropping that sense of self, we can release into the flow that is awen (a Welsh word used in Druidry, meaning inspiration), that is life and inspiration itself, flowing through space and time. It is a chance to connect with the earth, with deity, with everyone and everything on the planet, instead of just your own sense of self. How wonderful is that?

I do not underestimate the significance of focusing on the self in order to improve one's life – change must come from within. However, there is so much more to the world than the little universe we create around our sense of self – a brilliant world full of myriad possibilities. Take for instance the shamanic ability to shape-change – we must first be able to drop our sense of self in order to take wing as the marsh harrier, or stalk a pheasant through the underbrush like a fox. On a broader level, we can simply place our hands on the earth and feel all of life humming from this planet, but first we must silence the chattering self within if we are to listen and to hear it fully with an open heart.

To be able to open ourselves up to the grander scheme of things, we must find a place where we are held, where it is easy for us to open up our nemeton and let go into the unknown. Creation of a sacred space is key for some – whether we physically create a space or whether we simply expand our own nemeton to that with which we would connect, with honour and respect. We must first know where our edges are before we can release them and step over them into the unknown.

In Zen, it is acknowledged that the sense of self is an illusion – it is made up of the opinions and experiences that resonate the most strongly within us, that we wish to cultivate, or which touch us on such a deep soul level. Yet these are all attachments, which we must release in order to fully connect with the world at large. In *The Ten Bulls*, the seeker finally does manage to let go, to become one with everything, but more importantly, he then takes that back into the world and works in the world with that knowledge. Releasing into the void in order to connect fully takes great courage, great time and great skill. Yet it is so simple that it feels impossible. (See bibliography for more information on *The Ten Bulls*.)

This is where discipline is key. We must make the time if we truly do want to do this. We must want it with all our heart and soul. In Zen, there is a saying that you must want it as much as a man whose head is held under water wants air. If you want it that much, you will make the time. Nemetona, like sanctuary, will not come to you; you must seek Her out.

Stepping away from the loudness and hectic pace of our modern lives we can find the time to simply "be". We aren't human beings most of the time; we are human doings. We must relearn that art of simply being which can then connect us to everything else. Once we simply "are", then that sense of self fades away and the multitudes of awen around us are allowed to flow into and around us – we hear what in Druidry is known as "the song".

Take a micro-retreat, once a day, several times a day. Watch the sun rise and the sun set, and let go into that experience. The world is so much larger than you – why not experience it wholly and with reverence and honour? Weaving those dropped threads, you will become an integral part of the tapestry of life once again, and not just a loose thread dangling in the wind. Not going with the flow, but being the flow itself.

Marvellous.

Appendix IV

The Importance of Ritual

Is ritual important? Many Druids perform ritual on a fairly regular basis – at least the seasonal rituals that celebrate the turning of the wheel of the year. Many also honour the phases of the moon, in whatever aspect, whether it be quarter, half, full or new. There are also some for whom daily ritual gives special meaning to their lives and their loves – the rising or setting of the sun and moon, for instance, or saying a prayer of thanksgiving or a blessing before partaking of food and drink. But is it all that important?

I suppose that it is all based on the personal relationship to the natural world around us. For some, daily ritual helps to connect with the rhythms of life that might not otherwise be apparent – say, for example, if you are living in the city, and it's hard to hear the blackbirds at dusk above the din of rush-hour traffic, or you aren't able to see the sun or moon rise due to buildings blocking the view. For others a daily ritual isn't that important, for they already feel much more connected simply in their living circumstances – for instance, fellow author and blogger Nimue Brown lived on a narrowboat and was very much connected to, and at the mercy of, mother nature. It's akin to a friendship, in a sense – sometimes your friend lives far away, and you have to make a special effort to keep in contact with her. Sometimes your friend lives right next door, and it's much easier to keep in touch.

In Zen, regular daily practise of sitting meditation carries through into other aspects of our lives, where we bring awareness into everything, and in doing so take away the illusionary drama and seeing reality for the wondrous gift that it is. It requires discipline, however – to sit through the boredom, to sit when we don't feel like it, to be aware when we'd rather be daydreaming. Yet this discipline is, as I have found out, necessary for clarity.

At the time of writing, I haven't meditated for a week now, and I am feeling the difference. That daily ritual, of sitting down and spending half an hour each and every day in awareness really did permeate into the rest of my life. I didn't become lost in attachments to emotions – I still had feelings, but they didn't linger and cause as much suffering as before. When taking the time out to stop and meditate and be aware for a designated point each day was given up, those attachments came creeping back in. I was spending more and more time in my own head rather than in the real world.

Druid ritual can do the same for us, in keeping us connected to our spirituality, whatever our circumstances. Too easily we can become lost in our own worlds, realities that we have created out of our emotions and thoughts. Ritual can say, "Hey, look – enough. Stop. Look at what's really going on around you. Hear the stag calling. Hear the aeroplane. Watch the sun rise. The world is more than just you."

With Druid ritual, we gain inspiration from the natural world around us. That is what Awen is – an insight into nature, the nature of the world around us and our own human nature in turn. By doing Druid ritual we take the time to pause, to reflect, to take in that inspiration so that we may exhale it with love and compassion back into the world.

So, is ritual important? I think so – for ritual keeps us from taking things for granted. It brings awareness and that magic back into our mundane lives no matter what our circumstances are. No matter where we are in life, taking a moment to stop and simply be in the moment can help us gain inspiration and insight, as well as the opportunity to give back with thanks for all our blessings that we receive in this equally mundane and magical world.

Appendix V

Maiden Goddesses

I have always loved Maiden Goddesses, in their many forms. When I first started learning other mythologies from around the world as a child, it was the image of Artemis that struck me the most – a glorious, strong young woman with her bow, surrounded by wild animals under a waxing crescent moon. Someone who knows what they want and yet keeps it to themselves, guarding their bodies and sense of self and opening only to those they choose to love – the Maiden's love was not unconditional. She ran through the forest with muddy feet and wild hair, in skins and with fetishes dangling in the breeze. She still does.

As I near forty, the sensible part of me tells me that I should at least be looking into the Mother or Queen Goddesses, before I turn to face the Crone. The Maiden in me tells her to bog off.

It's in the waxing time that I long to dance and sing, that the energy is rising, when my blood stirs with passion. I love that crescent that hangs in the sky, a silver arc of glory and strength, bending but not breaking, supple and strong. The full moon does, of course, sing to me as well, as does the waning and new moon – I honour all the tides and times as they flow through this life and through me, connecting me with everything. Autumn is my favourite season – not a time of the Maiden, you might say – but the Maiden would say otherwise, for this is hunting season for us humans, when she and the Lord of the Wildwood watch over both predator and prey.

I suppose that being childless by choice has much to do with my perspective on the Maiden. She is free, unburdened, yet still carrying great responsibility. She is not naïve, she is not immature – for me she is strong-willed and determined. She is not innocence and unknowing – she is a Goddess after all, remember. She likes children but sees no need to have her own, for it does not fit in with her plans.

I don't seek a Mother Goddess, perhaps because I have never felt the need for one. My own physical mother provides me with that love that only a mother can. I personally don't believe in an all-loving Mother Goddess anyway – the Goddess as nature for me could never be so. Nature doesn't give two hoots about humanity.

Even my Lady Nemetona, much like the antlered goddess Elen, is not a mother-type figure. Nemetona provides us with that space where we can be, where our soul truth can sing. However, she is not motherly in the way that she provides it. She allows for that space to be – like a priest, she facilitates the power within and without to allow that time for growth, or reflection, or whatever it is that you seek. It is up to you to use it correctly. She watches over sacred sites, stone circles and deep lakes, mountaintops and dark caves where people have come for millennia, or for a season, to make ritual and connect with that which the Druids call awen. She holds a space, indeed she may hold us for a time, but it is so that we can better understand ourselves and the world, rather than out of any love. She is sometimes paired with the god Mars, sometimes with Mercury and Louceticus. However, simply because names are shared on an altar, it does not a couple make! At Bath, Nemetona and Mars also share temple space with Diana, Sulis and the local spirits, or genio loci and Sul/Minerva. For me, Nemetona is a Celtic goddess, and Mars most definitely a Roman god. It is well known that the Romans incorporated local deity worship alongside their own pantheon.

She has always made herself known to me to be a Maiden Goddess, true to herself, aware of her boundaries and setting them clearly. Others might see her differently. The Crone awaits me in the dark depths of winter, and perhaps one day I will seek her out. However, I have a feeling that the Maiden will still be at my side, forever and always running with me through forest and field under the bright sunshine, holding the sacred space, allowing us to shoot our bows deep into the heart of consciousness and forever sing under the light of the waxing moon.

Appendix VI

A Note on Authenticity vs Validity

I thought I should include here a note on authenticity vs validity. It is a discussion that comes up often with Pagan circles. With a book dedicated to such a little known deity, we can often seem to be "making it up as we go along". This experience, however, should not be diminished simply because it lacks historical corroboration.

I remember, quite a few years ago now, reading Ronald Hutton's *Triumph of the Moon*. I had always known, vaguely, that modern Paganism was just that – modern. After reading that book and finding out just how modern most of our rituals and celebrations are, I had a bit of a religious crisis. I was having a really hard time coming to terms with the fact that the spiritual path I was following was essentially made up by two guys in the 1950s and 60s.

For a couple of weeks I toiled with this issue, until it finally dawned on me that all religions, at some point, were made up by, or interpreted by, some people. Simply because someone made it up 200, 2,000 or 20,000 years ago didn't make it any more valid. I realised that authenticity did not equal validity.

There was no way of tracing Pagan roots back to what we would imagine to be a more "Pagan time" – i.e. for most this would be before Christianity. Paganism didn't write or record much down in words, though we can catch remnants in snatches of old folk songs, rhymes and the like. If our Paganism is inspired by an even older spirituality, such as that of our Neolithic ancestors, then certainly we have no written records – a few artefacts, burial mounds and sacred sites to draw inspiration on, but nothing of their words to live by. We still do not know, and can never be certain, what they actually believed, how they lived their lives and how they communed with their gods, if any. We can only speculate.

And so, two men, Gerald Gardner and Ross Nichols pieced together a spirituality as best they could, after looking into folk traditions and seeking inspiration from the natural world itself. This evolved into what is recognised as Wicca and Druidry today. These paths are not hundreds of years old, though they have been inspired by older traditions. This does not invalidate them in any way.

I would personally have a harder time believing in the validity of someone's path who told me that they were following a "thousands of years old British tradition" than someone who told me that they made up their own spiritual path. Why? Because the need for justification of a tradition bothers me – why do we need to justify our paths? Our good Druid friend, Iolo Morganwg, made up a lot of stuff when he couldn't find any reference to it a couple of hundred years ago,yet the stuff that he made up has great resonance and beauty for some Druids. Yes, he passed it off as "real", and was only caught out fairly recently in his forgeries. However, they still remain beautiful and meaningful forgeries nonetheless for many. It bothers me that he felt the need to forge these documents, but it doesn't make his tradition any less valid for himself and others whom it inspires. The question of lying about the authenticity of a tradition is what invalidates it for many.

Why do we feel the need to authenticate a religion or spiritual path before we embark upon it? Does this have anything to do with the Age of Enlightenment vs the Age of Reason? Why should one be more valid than the other, simply because it has hard facts that it can draw upon?

A religious and spiritual path is such a personal thing, that I find it hard to believe that any one path is good for more than one person. We can certainly be inspired by it, but the path must be walked by us, and us alone – no one else can do it for us.

Buddha said, "Be a light unto thyself." We have to find our own ways of communing, our own relationship with the world in order for it to make full sense to our hearts, bodies, minds and souls. Oftentimes the words and teachings of others can come close, and yet they are still not quite as personal as a one-to-one relationship.

Protestants have a more personal relationship with God, for the most part, than Catholics when it comes down to it. That is an inherent part of Protestantism, one that is explored and made quite poignant in Arthur Miller's *The Crucible*. Protestantism placed a great emphasis on personal, individual reading of the Bible, thereby increasing the personal relationship with God – no other could really do that for you. (Sadly, within history and especially after the birth of Calvinism, fundamentalism became de rigeur.)

How much of our Paganism today is influenced by this Protestant way of thinking? It's hard to tell, but it's not something I have a problem with. I like the idea of everyone having to find their own personal relationship with God, or a god, or goddess, or the spirits of place, their ancestors or the three worlds of land, sea and sky. This idea is, of course, not solely attributed to Protestantism (remember Buddha's quote?) but as it is one of the more recent religious institutions in the UK, we are currently exploring the legacy.

How far back the tradition of personal relationship with deity goes is, to me, of no consequence. It's nice to have historical authenticity, but it does not a spirituality make. What matters in life is the personal relationship you have with that with which you are communing. It changes you, inspires you, or moves you to what really matters in life. Whether you pray using a prayer that is a thousand years old, or one that you made up on the spot, it is in the feeling and intent behind it that matters most, not in the words themselves. It must connect you with what it is you are trying to reach, else what is the point?

So, to all those out there who are making it up as they go along, who find spiritual validity in what they do, I give a hearty hail! To those whose find the words of others resonate deeply within their soul, and blend their historic traditions with personal experience, again I give a hearty hail! Life is too short to follow a path simply because others have trodden it – we can learn from that path, but ultimately it is we who are doing the walking, no one else, and in this we find our own validity and personal experience blessing us along the way.

Bibliography

Carr- Gomm, P. (2002) *Druid Mysteries: Ancient Wisdom for the 21st Century,* Rider

Harris, I. (2004) *The Laughing Buddha of Tofukuji: The Life of Zen Master Keido Fukishima,* World Wisdom

Hutton, R. (2011) *Blood and Mistletoe: The History of the Druids in Britain,* Yale University Press

Hutton, R. (1999) *The Triumph of the Moon: A History of Modern Pagan Witchcraft,* Oxford Paperbacks

Restall Orr, E. (2004) *Living Druidry: Magical Spirituality for the Wild Soul,* London: Piatkus Books Ltd

Restall Orr, E. (1998) *Principles of Druidry,* Thorsons

Restall Orr, E. (2000) *Ritual: A Guide to Life, Love & Inspiration,* London: Thorsons

Internet Resources

The British Druid Order: www.druidry.co.uk

The Druid Network: druidnetwork.org

The Order of Bards, Ovates and Druids: www.druidry.org

The Ten Bulls: www.sacred-texts.com/bud/mzb/oxherd.htm

Suggested Reading

Brown, N. (2012) *Druidry and the Ancestors: Finding our Place in our History*, Moon Books

Brown, N. (2012) *Druidry and Meditation*, Moon Books

Billington, P. (2011) *The Path of Druidry: Walking the Ancient Green Way*, Llewellyn

Carr- Gomm, P. (2002) *Druid Mysteries: Ancient Wisdom for the 21st Century*, Rider

Carr-Gomm, P. (2002) *In the Grove of the Druids: The Druid Teachings of Ross Nichols*, Watkins Publishing

Hopman, E. E. (2008) *Priestess of the Forest: A Druid Novel*, Llewellyn

Hutton, R. (2011) *Blood and Mistletoe: The History of the Druids in Britain*, Yale University Press

Hutton, R. (1999) *The Triumph of the Moon: A History of Modern Pagan Witchcraft*, Oxford Paperbacks

Ly de Angeles et al (2005) *Pagan Visions for a Sustainable Future*, Llewellyn

Restall Orr, E. (2004) *Living Druidry: Magical Spirituality for the Wild Soul*, London: Piatkus Books Ltd

Restall Orr, E. (1998) *Principles of Druidry*, Thorsons

Restall Orr, E. (2000) *Ritual: A Guide to Life, Love & Inspiration*, London: Thorsons

Restall Orr, E. (1998) *Spirits of the Sacred Grove: The World of a Druid Priestess*, Llewellyn

Talboys, G.K. (2011) *The Druid Way Made Easy*, O Books

Treadwell, C. (2012) *A Druid's Tale*, John Hunt Publishing

van der Hoeven, J. (2013) *Zen Druidry: Living a Natural Life, with Full Awareness*, Moon Books

About the Author

Joanna van der Hoeven was born in Quebec, Canada, in the Laurentian mountains. She grew up on the edge of a small town, with her best friends the miles of forest that stretched behind her house and the horses in the fields below by the river. Her love of hiking and camping stemmed from childhood holidays, when she and her family would go to Mont Tremblant National Park and set up the tent for a week. Her fondest childhood memories are of listening to the loons on the lake at sunset, and climbing to the mountain's summit to see the old, rounded volcanic hills spread out in all directions, with trees and lakes as far as the eye could see.

Joanna's first ventures into Paganism were through Wicca, where she practised as a solitary in her college days in Montreal at the age of eighteen. She studied Wicca for ten years before coming to Druidry in her late twenties. Joanna moved to the United Kingdom and discovered the songs of the Emerald Isles, and the language that flowed with it, of pure awen. She began her studies in Druidry and for many years practised alone, with the wind and the trees, the seasons and old stories as her guides.

Joanna joined The Druid Network and began learning from Emma Restall Orr on her Living Druidry course, set over a year's cycle in the beautiful Cotswolds countryside with other students. She complemented her own studies with practical work under the guidance of Bobcat's tutelage, and went deeper into the Druid tradition. Joanna also took the Order of Bards, Ovates and Druids correspondence course. She continues to study as much as she can, learning not only from books and people but also from the land around her, her spirit guides and animal allies.

Joanna now lives in Suffolk, and continues her work in Druidry by working for charities, writing and acting as a priest for her local community. She sings back to the land where she lives, letting the awen flow. She cares a great deal about the land upon which she lives, and has a special affinity for animals of all kinds. She enjoys hiking and camping, and has interests in theology and art.

She is also a poet, musician, dancer and writer. She has written three books, *Instinct and Inspiration*, *Falconwing* and *Zen Druidry*. She has also written many articles for The Druid Network, writes the main blog for Moon Books, has another blog for the SageWoman channel at witchesandpagans.com as well as her own personal blog at www.octopusdance.wordpress.com.

Joanna is the Director of Gypsy Dreams Belly Dance, a fusion dance company in Suffolk that holds classes, workshops and events performing throughout the UK.

For more information about the author, please see the website at www.autumnsong.org.

Other Books by the Author

Zen Druidry: Living a Natural Life, with Full Awareness, Moon Books.

Taking both Zen and Druidry and embracing them into your life can be a wonderful and ongoing process of discovery, not only of the self but of the entire world around you. Looking at ourselves and at the natural world around us, we realise that everything is in constant change and flux – like waves upon the ocean, they are all part of one thing that is made up of everything. Even after the wave has crashed upon the shore, the ocean is still there, the wave is still there – it has merely changed its form. This text shows you how Zen teachings and Druidry can combine to create a peaceful life path that is completely and utterly dedicated to the here and now, to the earth and her rhythms and to the flow that is life itself.

MOON
BOOKS

Moon Books invites you to begin or deepen your encounter with
Paganism, in all its rich, creative, flourishing forms.